26th September, 1580

The *Golden Hinde* sails back into Plymouth.

1588

Drake takes part in the attack on the Spanish Armada at Calais. The Spanish are defeated.

1581

The *Golden Hinde* is put into dry dock for safe keeping by order of Queen Elizabeth I.

1596

Drake becomes ill with dysentery on a voyage and dies. He is buried at sea.

Hello, I am Queen Elizabeth of England. The year is 1577. My father was King Henry VIII and my mother was Anne Boleyn (wife number two). My parents' relationship was not good and my father had my mother beheaded when I was three. The Pope, the head of the Catholic Church in Rome, refused to recognise my father's divorce from his first wife, Catherine of Aragon. This meant that his marriage to my mother was not considered legal. So, for a time this made me illegitimate and I could not be heir to the throne. To overcome the Pope's refusal to recognise his divorce from Catherine, my father created a new branch of the Christian church – the Protestant Church of England.

When my father died, my half brother Edward, who was brought up in the Protestant faith, became king. He was always sickly and died aged just 16. Then my half-sister, Mary Tudor, became Queen. She was a Roman Catholic like her Spanish mother, Catherine of Aragon. Mary married the Spanish Prince Philip who would eventually become King Philip II of Spain. For a time Philip lived in England but as Mary did not produce an heir, he left. Mary is remembered in history as 'Bloody Mary' for her persecution of Protestants. Between 1555 and 1558, she ordered about 300 Protestants to be burned at the stake. On Mary's death, I became the Queen in 1558.

I have worked hard to be a popular Queen. Under my rule England is enjoying a golden age of exploration, art, music and literature. It is 85 years since Christopher Columbus sailed to the New World and discovered the 'West Indian'(Caribbean) islands. Between 1492 and 1504 Spain conquered the Aztec Empire, then moved south to conquer Peru and the west coast of Chile. Spain has grown rich from gold and silver mines in the New World, and her 'treasure ships' carry vast wealth home to Spain. If I can disrupt Spain's power there, I can take some of this wealth for England!

Spices worth more than their weight in gold come from the East by a long overland journey. For years there has been talk of a shorter sea route, the so called 'North West Passage' to the 'Spice Islands'. The country that finds this route, if it exists, will be very powerful indeed. Francis Drake is the right commander for this expedition! His reputation as a pirate is the perfect cover for the voyage. If anything goes wrong I will deny everything to avoid a war with Spain.

By the way, there were as many executions of Catholics in your reign, your Majesty, as there were of Protestants under Mary Tudor.
(Editor)

Author:
David Stewart has written many non-fiction books for children on historical topics, including *You Wouldn't Want To Be An Egyptian Mummy* and *You Wouldn't Want To Sail On The Titanic*. He lives in Brighton with his wife and son.

Artist:
David Antram was born in Brighton, England, in 1958. He studied at Eastbourne College of Art and then worked in advertising for fifteen years before becoming a full-time artist. He has illustrated many children's non-fiction books.

Series Creator:
David Salariya was born in Dundee, Scotland. He has illustrated a wide range of books and has created and designed many new series for publishers both in the UK and overseas. In 1989, he established The Salariya Book Company. He lives in Brighton with his wife, illustrator Shirley Willis, and their son Jonathan.

Consultant:
Stuart Slade read film and literature at Warwick University and gained a postgraduate diploma in Museum Studies at the University of Leicester in 1991. He has worked as Education Officer at the National Maritime Museum since 1998, developing a range of programmes and resources for primary, secondary and college groups, including many on Tudor exploration.

Editor: **Karen Smith**

PAPER FROM SUSTAINABLE FORESTS

Published in Great Britain in MMXIX by Book House, an imprint of
The Salariya Book Company Ltd
25 Marlborough Place, Brighton BN1 1UB
www.salariya.com

ISBN: 978-1-912904-08-2

SALARIYA
SCRIBO BOOK HOUSE SCRIBBLERS

© The Salariya Book Company Ltd MMXIX

1 3 5 7 9 8 6 4 2

A CIP catalogue record for this book is available from the British Library.
Printed and bound in China.

Visit
www.salariya.com
for our online catalogue and
free fun stuff.

You Wouldn't Want to Explore With Sir Francis Drake!

Be warned: if anyone hits a shipmate, they will lose a hand!

Written by
David Stewart

Illustrated by
David Antram

Created and designed by
David Salariya

A Pirate You'd Rather Not Know

BOOK HOUSE
a SALARIYA imprint

Contents

Introduction

It is 1577 and Francis Drake, the Queen of England's favourite adventurer, has been ordered to command a new expedition leaving from Plymouth. You are Francis Fletcher, a young preacher. You have heard stories about Drake's raids on ships in the Spanish Main. Drake is a deeply religious man and you have the good luck to be appointed as Chaplain to the expedition. You believe you are off on a trading trip to Alexandria in Egypt, but Drake's expedition has another purpose.

Where will this voyage take you? You will return from your journey nearly three years later a well-travelled and wiser man. But you would certainly avoid sailing with Francis Drake again!

I am Francis Drake, some say I am a pirate!

Pirate or privateer?

Francis Fletcher

YOU ARE A GRADUATE of Cambridge University and a keen traveller. You've already visited Russia, Spain and the Mediterranean.

I am Francis Fletcher. I plan to make notes in my journal of the voyage.

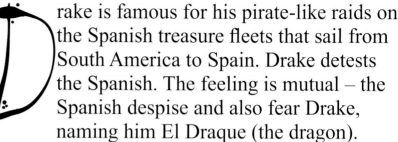

Drake is famous for his pirate-like raids on the Spanish treasure fleets that sail from South America to Spain. Drake detests the Spanish. The feeling is mutual – the Spanish despise and also fear Drake, naming him El Draque (the dragon). Philip II, the King of Spain, suspects that Drake is a privateer. This would mean that Drake's raids are approved by the Queen and that the Queen profits from them. Little do you know that the huge cost of this new expedition may well be covered by such acts of piracy.

The Spanish treasure fleets

THE 'TREASURE FLEETS' sail twice a year from Spain, carrying provisions, food, clothing, wine, oil and tools to South America. On the return journey the ships are loaded with silver and gold mined by slaves.

MEXICO

Caribbean Sea

SOUTH AMERICA

Handy hint

Sail with an experienced captain. Drake has made many voyages.

The Spanish Main

THE SPANISH TREASURE FLEET must sail through the Spanish Main on their voyages between the New World and Spain. Pirates are attracted to this region by these rich ships and the numerous islands and bays to hide in.

DRAKE comes from a family of seafarers. Long ago, William Hawkins, Drake's uncle, showed King Henry VIII exotic fruit he had brought back from his travels.

So, these coconuts, bananas and oranges — what do you do with them?

The Queen's secret plans

Investors have planned an expedition which some say is in search of the Northwest Passage, a possible sea route between the Atlantic and Pacific Oceans. Drake has chosen the *Pelican* as his flagship, a 120-tonne, 18-gun ship with a double hull, built with Drake's own money. One hundred and sixty-four men and boys make up the crew, some of whom have invested money in the expedition. Drake himself has invested £1,000.

On 15th November, 1577, the *Pelican* sails from Plymouth with four other ships: the *Elizabeth*, the *Marigold*, the *Swan* and the *Benedict*. However, wild storms soon force the ships back to Plymouth and some are badly damaged. On 13th December the expedition sets sail once more for the Moroccan island of Mogador.

The real purpose of the expedition is revealed!

LIKE MOST OF THE CREW, you think you are on a trading mission to Alexandria. On reaching the coast of Africa, your destination changes.

YOUR REAL DESTINATION is the Pacific Ocean via the Strait of Magellan to find the Northwest Passage – the route to the Far East and the fabled Spice Islands.

SOME OF THE CREW are not happy about the change of plan. Of course, if you can raid the Spanish treasure fleet and disrupt the wealth flowing to Spain, that would be helpful too.

YOUR SMALL FLEET CAPTURES a Portuguese ship near São Tiago in the Cape Verde Islands. One of the prisoners, Nuño De Silva, is an experienced navigator. When he hears where you are going he chooses to come with you. He has useful maps and charts which are more valuable than gold to Drake.

This is Diego, Drake's manservant. To find out more about him, go to page 38.

It's the charts that are important...

Handy hint

Aching and swollen joints? Bad breath? Bleeding gums? Teeth falling out? You have scurvy! Eat plenty of fresh fruit.

Island of blood

Storms separate the ships on the South American coast. Anchoring at Port St. Julian, the crew are uneasy. This is where the explorer Magellan once hanged a sailor for mutiny and marooned two others. Thomas Doughty has been trying to undermine Drake's authority. Doughty is accused of plotting against Drake and is brought to trial. Drake decides that only three vessels will now sail on from Port St. Julian: the *Pelican*, now re-named the *Golden Hinde*, the *Marigold* and the *Elizabeth*. On 17th August, 1578, the ships set sail for the Strait of Magellan.

TALES OF MAGELLAN'S CRUELTY to the native people 58 years earlier have not been forgotten. The native people are not friendly (left). Your gunner and the surgeon are killed in a fight.

CAPTURED during another raid, the *Mary* is too rotten to use any more. The ship is broken up and used as firewood (right).

THE CREW SPEND THEIR TIME 'CAREENING' – scraping barnacles and seaweed off the hull to prevent them slowing the ship down (left). Drake is very careful about the maintenance of his ships.

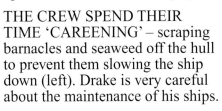

THE COOPER from the *Pelican* makes tankards (right) from the old gibbet used by explorer Magellan to hang his mutinous crew member.

Lo! This is the end of traitors!

Handy hint

Sea lion oil is good for curing pimples. Eat mussels and seaweed stew, to give you strength!

Re-naming the flagship

The *Pelican* is re-named the *Golden Hinde* on 21st August, 1578, in honour of Sir Christopher Hatton, whose crest featured a 'hinde', a female deer. Thomas Doughty was employed by Hatton as a private secretary. Drake is thinking ahead to a time when he'll have to explain Doughty's execution.

AT HIS TRIAL, 40 MEN on the jury find Thomas Doughty guilty and he is sentenced to death for mutiny. Doughty chooses to die under the axe.

15

Storms hit the fleet

Golden Hinde's route

NORTH AMERICA

Atlantic Ocean

AFRICA

Peru

SOUTH AMERICA

Precise route unknown!

After sailing through the Strait of Magellan safely, fierce storms rage in the Pacific for two months. The fleet hugs the coast of South America. Drake tries to keep the ships together but they become separated. The *Golden Hinde* is blown far to the south. The *Marigold* sinks in the storm with all on board. Drake thinks the *Elizabeth* is lost too. Fifty-two days after the ships have passed through the Strait of Magellan, a course is set to sail northwest towards Peru.

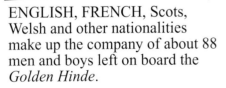

ENGLISH, FRENCH, Scots, Welsh and other nationalities make up the company of about 88 men and boys left on board the *Golden Hinde*.

DRAKE BELIEVES the *Elizabeth* is lost in the storms. She was blown back to the Strait of Magellan and sails for England where she arrives safely.

THREE THOUSAND penguins are slaughtered by the crew – enough meat for 40 days.

16

THE *Marigold* sinks in the storms, with all on board. You believe this is God's punishment for the ship's Master. He was one of Thomas Doughty's accusers.

Handy hint

To keep the hull watertight, paint it with hot tar and brimstone.

17

The calm after the storms

The *Golden Hinde* sails north into the Spanish-owned waters of Peru. When stopping for food at the island of Mocha, angry natives mistake the English for their Spanish oppressors and attack. Drake is hit twice. One man has 21 arrows in him and another dies from his wounds. Drake raids the Spanish settlements and takes his biggest prize, the treasure ship *Cacafuego*. Drake tells her captain, San Juan de Anton, the real purpose of his expedition. The Spanish authorities are furious. They know that if Drake finds the 'Strait of Bacallaos' (the Northwest Passage) and sets up a colony, no Spanish ship will ever be safe again.

Raids!

DRAKE'S RAIDS on the Spanish settlements cause little harm to the Spanish or the native people (left).

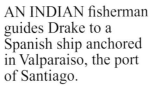

AN INDIAN fisherman guides Drake to a Spanish ship anchored in Valparaiso, the port of Santiago.

PORT CALLAO at Lima was founded in 1535. It is the centre of Spain's colonial administration so is ideal for a raid (left).

SILVER, extracted by slaves from the nearby mines of Potosi, is sent to Arica, so there are rich pickings to be had (right).

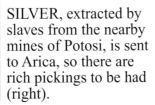

The Cacafuego

THE CAPTURED SHIP is carrying 1,300 bars of silver, weighing 26 tonnes, 13 chests of silver coins and 36 kilograms of gold. Some of this treasure belongs to the King of Spain.

CAPTAIN SAN JUAN DE ANTON is slashed across the face by a crossbow and Drake cleans and dresses the wound himself. Drake then releases Anton, his passengers and crew, giving them 30 to 40 pesos each.

Plundering treasure ships

The *Cacafuego* and her crew are set free and the *Golden Hinde* sails 960 kilometres in nine days along the west coast of New Spain (now Central America). Anchored near the island of Caño, the crew enjoys fresh meat for the first time in a month, including monkey and alligator! With treasure piling up in the hold, Drake is on the look-out for another ship to share the load. The *Capitiana* is captured along with its useful navigation charts for a route to Manila in the Philippines. Barnacles are building up on the *Golden Hinde*'s hull which slow her down. She needs to be careened but a partial clean up has to do. A few weeks later Spanish nobleman Don Francisco de Zárate's ship is sighted.

Please don't take my clothes, they are very expensive.

AT DUSK on 3rd April Zárate's ship is sighted on the horizon. The crew board her at dawn and find her full of riches.

THE SHIP IS LADEN with linen, chests full of fine china dishes and oriental silks.

ZÁRATE is finely dressed and pleads with Drake not to take his expensive clothes. Drake takes nearly everything else, including the passengers' trunks!

ZÁRATE IS INVITED TO DINE with Drake on the *Golden Hinde* and later reports that the food was served on 'silver dishes given to Drake by the Queen'. He also reports that Drake is 'about 35 years of age...with a fair beard, and is one of the greatest mariners that sails the seas'. When Drake escorts Zárate back to his ship, he leaves the Portugese pilot behind, too.

Handy hint

To persuade a captured pilot to steer your ship through unknown waters, threaten to hang him.

Here's to the Queen of England, God bless her.

Making repairs

Drake's small fleet sails west and then north. By mid July the ships are in need of repair so a safe harbour must be found. They anchor in a bay which Drake names 'Nova Albion', Latin meaning 'New England'. The native people here seem peaceful. Some of the crew go hunting with the native people and discover they are very skillful with bows and arrows.

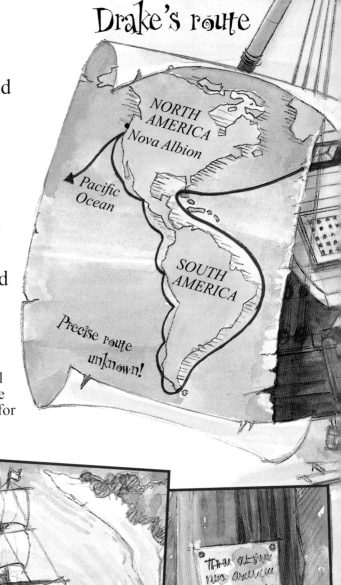

Drake's route

NORTH AMERICA
Nova Albion

Pacific Ocean

SOUTH AMERICA

Precise route unknown!

WHEN they return from the voyage, Drake and his men tell many different stories of where they had been. No one knows for sure where Nova Albion was.

Nova Albion

THE *GOLDEN HINDE* is leaking. It is bitterly cold and too stormy to go further north in search of the Northwest Passage.

THE SHIP takes refuge in the shallow bay they named Nova Albion so that vital repairs can be done.

FIVE WEEKS PASS in this safe harbour. Drake leaves an engraved brass plate nailed to a post, claiming the land for Queen Elizabeth.

The island of thieves

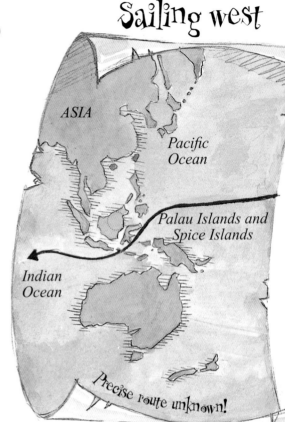

About 68 days after leaving the coast of America and 19,000 kilometres from England, the *Golden Hinde* finds land across the Pacific Ocean. The ship's company is down to 62 men and boys. After a fight with the Palau Islanders, they sail on. Local fishermen guide Drake to the Moluccas, known as the Spice Islands. When Sultan Babú of Ternate is told that Drake represents the Queen of England, he meets Drake's ship in a great royal canoe and his people tow it into harbour.

ASIA

Pacific Ocean

Palau Islands and Spice Islands

Indian Ocean

Precise route unknown!

WITH THE AID OF SPANISH CHARTS from captured ships, the *Golden Hinde* sails away from America and heads west across the Pacific.

IN THE PALAU ISLANDS, about 100 canoes full of native people come to trade coconuts, fish and fruit in return for beads. But the islanders then decide to take what they want from the ship. Hundreds more return. Drake fires a cannon and about 20 natives are killed.

Handy hint

Cloves and some spices from these islands can be worth their weight in gold.

Careful where you're firing that, Captain!

25

Sailing into trouble

The next destination is the island of Java, 1,600 kilometres further southwest, in the Indian Ocean. It is difficult to find a way through the many islands here and the *Golden Hinde* strikes a coral reef. She is stuck fast and the crew are worried.

As darkness falls the ship could be smashed to pieces on the reef. In the hope that the tide will free the ship next day, Drake orders the crew to lighten the ship. Food, cannons and tonnes of cloves worth a fortune are thrown overboard! Next day, at four in the afternoon, the tide lifts the ship off the reef.

CRRrunch!

DRAKE ORDERS YOU TO PRAY for them. Your sermon suggests that the disaster is God's punishment for the expedition's piracy and for the execution of Thomas Doughty. Drake is furious with you!

DRAKE ORDERS that you are to be tied up with a sign reading, 'Francis Fletcher, ye falseth knave that liveth'.

Homeward bound

You eventually reach Java, after strong winds blow the ship off course. You anchor on the south coast and send gifts to the local ruler, the raja. He gives you hens, coconuts and rice in return. Once again the ship is careened. You take on more supplies for the homeward journey – water, hens, goats, fruit and seven tonnes of rice! Portuguese spies find their way on board, taking notes on the state and contents of the *Golden Hinde*. Drake sets sail for the Cape of Good Hope.

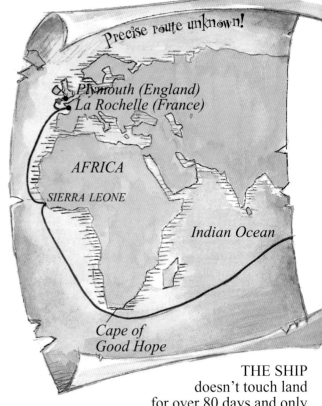

Precise route unknown!

Plymouth (England)
La Rochelle (France)

AFRICA

SIERRA LEONE

Indian Ocean

Cape of Good Hope

THE SHIP doesn't touch land for over 80 days and only just makes it to Sierra Leone before you all die of thirst.

Home at last!

DRAKE ANCHORS near La Rochelle, France. Some of the treasure is secretly unloaded – probably in case you get a hostile welcome in England for upsetting the Spanish so much!

THE *GOLDEN HINDE* finally sails back into Plymouth on 26th September, 1580. Drake is keen to find out if Queen Elizabeth is alive and still on the throne.

DRAKE'S WIFE, Mary, and the mayor of Plymouth come to see Drake on his ship. Messages are sent to the Queen in London, telling of his safe return.

29

Fame and riches

Francis Drake's navigational skills are extraordinary. Only Magellan had ever circumnavigated the globe before – and he died on his homeward journey! However, despite his success Queen Elizabeth keeps her distance from Drake. She knows that no sea captain has been more destructive to the Spanish empire. But she is curious to see Drake's treasure and spends hours with him hearing about the voyage. Eventually the treasure is taken to the Tower of London.

The Queen had invested £1,000 in the expedition and she receives £47,000 in return. Drake is allowed to keep £10,000. He buys a large estate, Bucklands Abbey, north of Plymouth.

Hurrumph!

THE TREASURE brought home to England is vast: it includes more than ten tonnes of silver and about 50 kilograms of gold. Drake took some treasure off his ships before landing in England, how much is unknown.

THE SPANISH are not happy about Drake's actions, especially as they seem to be approved by Queen Elizabeth. The King of Spain starts building an invincible fleet to fight the English. It will finally set sail in 1588.

footer-navigation 31

Final voyage

THE QUEEN GRANTS DRAKE his own coat of arms with the motto 'Sic parvis magna' – 'Greatness from small beginnings'.

What happens next...

Sir Francis Drake continues to fight the Spanish. In 1585 he holds the island of Sao Tiago to ransom and burns down its towns. His attacks on the ports of Cadiz and Corunna in Spain in 1587 become known as the 'singeing of the King of Spain's beard'. Over two days, Drake steals or sinks 38 ships at Cadiz. In 1588, Drake takes part in the attack on the Spanish Armada at Calais, led by Lord High Admiral Howard of Effingham. Bad weather forces the Armada back to Spain and many of their ships are wrecked in storms.

On Drake's final voyage in 1596, he is ill with dysentery for several days and dies at sea, off the coast of Panama. His body is placed in a lead coffin and buried at sea. He is about 54 years old.

QUEEN ELIZABETH officially recognises Drake's feat of circumnavigation. In 1581 she orders that the *Golden Hinde* be put in dry dock for safe keeping (opposite).

NOBODY KNOWS the full story of the voyage because it was so secret and many 'tall-tales' were told to make the sailors sound exciting and hide any crimes.

It's the Spanish Armada, Sir Francis!

Handy hint (for Drake)

Like Fletcher, produce a book based on your journal from the voyage. If it gives too much away it won't be published for years to come!*

*The World Encompassed by Sir Francis Drake is finally published in 1628.

31

Glossary

Brimstone The old word for sulphur.

Buccaneer A pirate who raided the Spanish-owned land and treasure fleets in South America and the Caribbean.

Careening To put a ship over on one side to clean or repair its hull.

Circumnavigate To sail completely around the world.

Colony A group of settlers in a new country.

Cooper A person who makes and repairs barrels.

Dysentery Disease causing severe diarrhoea.

Gibbet A wooden frame where executed criminals were hung for public viewing.

Magellan, Ferdinand A Portuguese explorer who attempted to circumnavigate the globe in 1519.

Mariner A seaman; a person who earns his living by going to sea.

Maroon To leave a person on an island and abandon them there. This was a punishment for mutinous crew members.

Mutiny A rebellion against those in authority, for example against the captain of a ship.

Navigator A person who can plot a route and direct a ship to follow that route.

New World The Americas.

Peso The currency of Spain.

Pilot A person who has the skill to guide a ship into and out of a port.

Pirate A person who robs from and steals ships.

Privateer A privately owned ship hired for war service by a government.

São Tiago One of the Cape Verde Islands off the west coast of Africa, under Spanish control.

Sermon A religious speech.

Spanish Main The southern part of the Caribbean Sea where Spanish treasure fleets sailed in the 16th and 17th centuries.

Surgeon A person on board a ship who looks after the sick and wounded.

Ternate One of the islands making up the Moluccas, or Spice Islands, between Celebes and New Guinea.

Index

The Spanish Armada

The King of Spain's plan to send a fleet of ships to invade England in 1588, partly in revenge for Drake's behaviour, was a complete disaster. The English ships had superior firepower and better gunners, and a very clever strategy for defeating the Spanish fleet. They sent blazing fireships towards the Spanish fleet, causing the Spanish ships to panic and scatter, many colliding with each other. The following morning, the Spanish ships engaged in battle with the English, but were outgunned. A storm blew in during the afternoon and the Spanish ships were pushed into the North Sea. As the Spanish fleet tried to flee back home, the bad weather blew many ships inshore off the coasts of England and Ireland, where many were smashed on the rocks. Only 65 of the 130 Spanish ships that sailed for England made it back home.

Diego and Drake

One crew member who travelled with Drake on his voyage from Plymouth had an extraordinary story of his own. Diego, whose surname is unknown, was an African slave who joined Drake and his men when they attacked Panama in Central America in 1572. Diego had wanted to escape slavery under the Spanish, and this was his chance to do so. He helped Drake to team up with other Africans who had run away from the Spanish, called the Cimaroons, and launch an attack on the enemy nation.

Diego was Drake's manservant on the Plymouth voyage, serving his meals and carrying out other tasks for him. Since the true nature of Drake's expedition was to seize Spanish and Portuguese shipping, Diego's ability to speak Spanish made him a valuable member of the crew, able to spy on the enemy. In 1578, Drake and his crew, including Diego, were attacked by the inhabitants of Mocha Isle, off the coast of Chile. Diego is said to have received more than 20 wounds in the attack. It's not clear from later records whether Diego eventually died from these wounds a year later, near the Indonesian Moluccas, or if he died at another later date for reasons unknown. Either way, he lived a very remarkable – and very dangerous – life.

Piracy facts

Ever since ships first sailed, pirates have attacked them. Pirate raids on ancient Egypt were reported almost 4,000 years ago. Greek and Roman pirates seized ships and passengers, Vikings looted Europe and Chinese gangs terrorised Asian seas. These early pirates set a pattern of robbery with violence that continues today.

Chinese pirates sailed in converted junks (cargo vessels). Their speed, cannons and big holds for storing gunpowder made them perfect for fighting. For hand-to-hand fighting, they favoured long, heavy swords that could slice through metal.

Edward Teach, born in Bristol, is much better known to us today by his pirate name of Blackbeard. His cruel ways and strange appearance, as presented by his first biographer Captain Charles Johnson in 1724, made him into a legend.

According to Johnson, whose account of Blackbeard was probably highly fanciful, the pirate was covered in pistols and daggers and shot his own crew on a whim. However, it is more likely that Blackbeard used fear rather than violence to get his way. He was said to terrify the crews on ships he plundered by tying lit fuses under his hat before boarding them.

The skull and crossbones on pirate flags were symbols understood by seamen of all nations. They stood for death and violence. Many prize ships surrendered when they saw them.